W9-BAS-904

A WORLD OF HOLIDAYS

Kwanzaa

A WORLD OF HOLIDAYS

Kwanzaa

Darwin McBeth Walton

RSVP

**RAINTREE
STECK-VAUGHN**
P U B L I S H E R S
A Steck-Vaughn Company

Austin, Texas

Published by Raintree Steck-Vaughn Publishers,
an imprint of Steck-Vaughn Company

Library of Congress Cataloging-in-Publication Data

Walton, Darwin McBeth.
    Kwanzaa / Darwin McBeth Walton.
       p.   cm. — (A world of holidays)
    Includes bibliographical references and index.
    Summary: Discusses the origins and symbols of Kwanzaa, the holiday that focuses on African American history, culture, and experiences, and offers suggestions for ways to celebrate this holiday.
    ISBN 0-8172-5561-3 (hardcover)
    ISBN 0-8172-8107-X (softcover)
    1. Kwanzaa — Juvenile literature.   2. Afro-Americans — Social life and customs — Juvenile literature.   [1. Kwanzaa. 2. Afro-Americans — Social life and customs.]   I. Title. II. Series.
GT4403.W36   1999
394.261 – dc21   98-9683
                            CIP   AC

Printed and bound in the United States
1 2 3 4 5 6 7 8 9 0 02 01 00 99 98

ACKNOWLEDGMENTS

Editors: Sabrina Crewe, Kathy DeVico
Design: Sabine Beaupré
Artwork: Ceci Graphics
Planned and produced by Discovery Books

For permission to reproduce copyright material, the authors and publishers gratefully acknowledge the following:

Front cover Lawrence Migdale
Title page Lawrence Migdale
Contents page Devendra Shrikhande
pages 6/7 Lawrence Migdale **pages 8/9** Schomburg Center for Research in Black Culture, The New York Public Library **page 10** (top) Lawrence Migdale, (bottom) The Hutchison Library **page 11** Edward Parker/The Hutchison Library **page 12** David Young-Wolff/PhotoEdit **page 13** Lawrence Migdale **page 14** Lawrence Migdale **page 15** Pat Olear/PhotoEdit **page 16** Lawrence Migdale **page 17** (left) Martha Brock, (right) Cindy Charles/PhotoEdit **page 18** (top) Lawrence Migdale, (bottom) Robert Brenner/PhotoEdit **page 19** Lawrence Migdale **page 20** Nancy Sheehan/PhotoEdit **page 21** (top) Lawrence Migdale, (bottom) Felicia Martinez/PhotoEdit **page 22** Billy E. Barnes/PhotoEdit **page 23** (left) David Young-Wolff/PhotoEdit, (right) Lawrence Migdale **page 24** (top) Lawrence Migdale, (bottom) Felicia Martinez/PhotoEdit **page 25** Lawrence Migdale **page 26** David Young-Wolff/PhotoEdit **page 27** Martha Brock **pages 28/29** Devendra Shrikhande

Contents

What Is Kwanzaa?

Imagine a holiday beginning the day after Christmas. Imagine seven days of celebration, filled with wonderful stories. Imagine making gifts and learning new songs. Millions of African American children and their families celebrate this holiday. It is called Kwanzaa!

A FAMILY HOLIDAY

Kwanzaa is not a religious holiday, such as Passover. Kwanzaa is a celebration of African American history and customs. Family traditions and good ways of behaving are important, too.

During Kwanzaa, a special table is set up. The table holds the things that are most important for Kwanzaa. Each day the family gathers around the table. Candles are lit at the beginning of the celebrations.

THE SEVEN PRINCIPLES

Kwanzaa lasts for seven days, beginning on December 26th and ending on January 1st. For each day of Kwanzaa there is a principle. These principles are rules to guide the celebration. The seven principles are called the Nguzo Saba. The Nguzo Saba help people to think about their lives and to remember their history.

On every day of Kwanzaa, families talk about that day's principle. They

Kwanzaa is a very important holiday for African Americans. It is celebrated in schools, in churches, and at special community events.

celebrate each day of the holiday in different ways. On the sixth day there is a big feast called Karamu, with music and dancing and lots of fun.

7

The African American Story

Some people may wonder why African Americans have a special holiday. It is because many African Americans believe it is important to celebrate their African history.

SLAVES FROM AFRICA

You have probably learned about slavery. So you know that African people were bought or kidnapped, and then brought to North America on ships. Most were sold as slaves to plantation owners in the southern part of the United States.

Slaves worked very hard on the plantations. They grew cotton, rice, sugarcane, and tobacco. They were not paid for their work and were often cruelly beaten. Slaves had no rights. Families were split up, and children were taken from their mothers.

These African people are on board a ship taking them to the United States. They were kept in chains and given just enough food to stay alive.

When African people became slaves in America, their customs and beliefs mixed with those of their owners. Their African way of living was mostly forgotten.

THE CIVIL WAR
Many free people living in the northern and eastern parts of the United States believed slaves should be freed. The disagreement between the North and the South over slavery was the main reason for the Civil War. The war lasted from 1861 to 1865. In 1865 the slaves were freed. But for a long time afterward, it was difficult for African Americans to vote or own land. They were kept apart from white people. They couldn't go to the same schools or visit many public places.

THE CIVIL RIGHTS ACT
In 1964 the most important Civil Rights Act was passed. It meant that every person had the same rights. The law said that African Americans had to be treated in the same way as everybody else.

Martin Luther King, Jr. believed that all people should be treated fairly. He gave his life to working for the rights of African American people.

The First Fruits

Kwanzaa was created in 1966 by Dr. Maulana Karenga. He believed it was time for African Americans to remember their African ancestors.

The man in the middle of this picture is Dr. Maulana Karenga. He believes that African Americans can make their lives better by keeping African customs alive.

Harvesting in Africa is often still done in traditional ways.

HARVESTTIME

The harvest has always been a time for celebration. In many parts of Africa, people celebrated harvesttime with a huge party. After gathering their crops, the families or community would come together. They would bring an offering of food from their harvest. Hunters also brought fish to bake and game to roast.

After the feast, people danced and sang, beat drums, and played other musical instruments. They gave thanks for their harvest and remembered their ancestors.

THE NGUZO SABA

Dr. Karenga used these African harvest traditions when he created Kwanzaa. He also used words from the African language Kiswahili. (Kiswahili is also called Swahili.) The word "Kwanzaa" comes from the Kiswahili phrase "matunda ya kwanza," which means "first fruits of the harvest."

The seven principles (the Nguzo Saba) all have Kiswahili names. These principles are called Umoja, Kujichagulia, Ujima, Ujamaa, Nia, Kuumba, and Imani.

When people meet during Kwanzaa, they greet each other with the words, "Habari gani?" That means, "What's new?" Then they answer with the name of that day's principle. The first day it would be "Umoja." On the last day, the reply would be "Imani."

African music, dancing, and art are all celebrated during Kwanzaa.

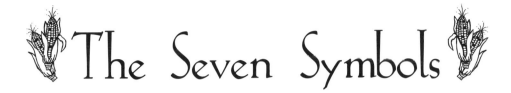

The Seven Symbols

Every family decorates their home for Kwanzaa with things that are special to them. But there are seven things that are always used. These are the symbols of Kwanzaa.

THE KWANZAA TABLE

The Mkeka is a straw mat that is placed on a table, over a brightly colored cloth. The table will hold all the symbols of Kwanzaa.

The Kwanzaa table is ready with all its symbols in place.

THE KINARA AND CANDLES

The Kinara plays a very important part in Kwanzaa. It is placed in the center of the Mkeka. The Kinara has seven holders that are filled with candles, one for each day. The candles are called the Mishumaa Saba. A black candle in the center stands for African American people.

The three green candles are symbols of new life. The three red candles stand for the blood of African ancestors.

HARVEST FRUITS

Muhindi is Kiswahili for ears of corn. One ear of corn for each child in the family is put on the table. The other fruits and vegetables on the table are the Mazao, the fruits of harvest. Pumpkins, squash, apples, nuts, roots, and grain are placed in bowls or baskets.

The Kikombe cha Umoja is a cup. It is also called the unity cup. Unity means being together. The unity cup is the symbol of family and community. The last symbol is the Zawadi. These are gifts that are given at Kwanzaa.

People try to keep Kwanzaa simple. Many things can be made by children and other family members.

13

Umoja

During Kwanzaa, candles are lit at the start of each day's celebrations. Often a child is chosen to light the candles. Every day, one more candle is lit. On the first day of Kwanzaa, only the black candle is lit.

THE MEANING OF UMOJA

The family gathers to talk about the principle of Umoja. Umoja is about being together and staying together. Each person has a chance to say what Umoja means to them. People talk of ways to keep their community and their family together. Children are encouraged to write to relatives in other cities, and send them photographs and cards.

On Umoja, families can look at photographs and remember their ancestors. They talk about the importance of staying together as a family.

THE LIBATION CEREMONY

The Libation Ceremony is usually done along with the lighting of the Umoja candle. A libation is a drink poured in honor of gods or ancestors. It helps everyone to remember family members who lived before them. The unity cup is filled with water, and a small amount is sprinkled onto the floor to honor African ancestors.

In some families each person has his or her own unity cup for the Libation Ceremony. Everyone drinks from their own cup at the same time.

Then the unity cup is passed around for all family members to take a sip. After the Umoja celebration, everybody shouts "Harambee!" which means, "Let's pull together!" The candle is blown out until the next day.

15

Kujichagulia

The principle for the second day means making your own decisions. People practice Kujichagulia by choosing who they want to be, and what they want to do for themselves.

THE SECOND DAY

The black candle on the Kinara is lit again. Then one of the red candles is lit. The family may decide to perform the Libation Ceremony. Each person can then say what Kujichagulia means to him or her. On this day, families try to find out about the talents and abilities of all their members.

Storytelling is important at Kwanzaa. Children can hear about their African roots. They learn about African American heroes and what they gave to the world.

When the Kujichagulia ceremony is completed, the family members shout "Harambee! Harambee!" Every day another "Harambee!" is added.

A famous woman who practiced Kujichagulia is Rosa Parks. Mrs. Parks was an important person in the Civil Rights movement during the 1950s and 1960s. Her courage helped other African American people to speak for themselves.

Making posters of the Nguzo Saba is a good way to remember the principles of Kwanzaa. The posters are used to decorate for the holiday.

LEARNING KUJICHAGULIA

Many schools around the country discuss the principles of Kwanzaa. When they think about Kujichagulia, students at school may talk about famous African Americans of the past. The class discusses the problems these people had to face. They learn about people who made brave choices. This makes them want to practice Kujichagulia themselves.

17

Ujima

Ujima means working together and looking after each other. This is the third day of Kwanzaa. It reminds families and the community to work toward what is best for everyone.

Trying on clothes for Kwanzaa can be fun. Boys wear colorful shirts called dashikis. Kufi hats can be bought or made at home.

Working together means that everyone can do things to help.

WORKING TOGETHER

The greeting of "Habari gani?" brings a cry of "Ujima!" Three candles are lit, and the family talks about the day's principle. They can find out about one another's problems, and help to solve them together.

18

The words to a song often sung on Ujima are:

When we all get together, together, together,
When we all work together, the happier we'll be.
For your friend is my friend, and my friend is your friend.
When we all play together, the happier we'll be.

CLOTHES FOR KWANZAA

On the third day of Kwanzaa, people could buy or make traditional African outfits. Many clothes are made from kente cloth. Kente cloth is a woven material that has been worn by African people for hundreds of years. Scarves made of this are worn by men and boys. Girls and women often wear beautiful bead necklaces and bracelets.

Women and girls wear dresses made with brightly patterned African cloth. Their head wraps are called gele.

Ujamaa

Ujamaa is the fourth principle of the Nguzo Saba. This day encourages African Americans to build their own places of work. It reminds people to shop at stores in their community and help other local businesses.

COMMUNITY SUPPORT

Four candles are lit. The unity cup is filled, and the Libation Ceremony takes place. The family may discuss how they can practice Ujamaa in their own neighborhood. They can decide to use local stores more often. They can plan to visit African American dentists and doctors.

Ujamaa also means sharing money in the community. This can be done by helping people in need.

Shopping for food can be done in neighborhood stores selling African and other foods. Many fresh vegetables are used in African American dishes.

FOOD FOR KWANZAA

On the fourth day of Kwanzaa, the family can start to prepare for the Karamu feast. Food is an important part of the celebration. There should be plenty to eat, and it should be beautifully cooked and served.

A MENU FOR KARAMU:

Baked or steamed fish
Roast pork or game meat
Greens, such as collards and kale
Okra, corn, and stewed tomatoes
Hoppin' John (black-eyed
 peas and rice)
Yams (sweet potatoes)
Corn bread and whole grain bread
Banana pudding and peach cobbler
Benne cakes (sesame cookies)
Fruits of all kinds

This big market is selling African goods. It gives the community a chance to support craftspeople and others in their neighborhood.

Cakes and cookies for Karamu can be made a few days ahead. This delicious peanut dish will be eaten at the feast.

Nia

The fifth day of Kwanzaa is Nia, which means purpose. Purpose is about making plans and having reasons for doing things. Nia encourages people to have goals that help build their neighborhood. It is also about building the whole African American community and making it strong.

MAKING PLANS

When five candles have been lit on the Kinara, each person talks about his or her plans for the future. They think about using their talents and abilities to reach their goals. Family members and friends might say how they can help make each other's dreams happen. They also discuss ways they could help improve the neighborhood, making it cleaner and safer for everyone.

Community gardens give people an opportunity to pratice Nia. Projects like this help the neighborhood and give everyone a sense of purpose.

Anyone can join in the musical performances with their own drum during Kwanzaa.

MAKING MUSIC

Getting ready for the next day's celebrations keeps everyone busy on the fifth day. Music will be a big part of the entertainment for the Karamu feast. Children can make rattles and drums to play during Kwanzaa. They can rehearse their songs and get ready to take part in the Karamu program.

This is an African drum made of carved wood and cloth. Drumming has always been important in African music, and it brings tradition and excitement to Kwanzaa.

Kuumba

The sixth day of Kwanzaa is a day to celebrate being creative. Music, dance, and art are especially important on Kuumba. It is also the day of the Karamu!

If there are many guests at the feast, children can sit on the floor at their own special table.

WELCOME TO THE FEAST

The mood of Kuumba is one of celebration. Guests arrive to join in the fun. Six candles are lit on the Kinara. Everybody joins in the Libation Ceremony. Many families spend time celebrating great African American artists.

Gourds and squash are used to decorate the Karamu feast.

Kukaribisha is the welcoming ceremony held before the feast. A member of the family makes a short speech about the meaning of Kwanzaa. Anyone who wants to ask a blessing or say a prayer may do so.

FOOD AND FUN

The table is filled with all kinds of delicious things to eat. People sit around the table, or on the floor in the traditional African style. The meal is a time for great fun as well as delicious food. The family and their guests make speeches, sing, and play music.

After dinner everybody stands for a farewell speech, read by the eldest member of the family. This shows that the feast and the year have come to an end.

After the feast, members of the family perform in the Karamu program. Children find many ways to be creative. They can read a poem, perform a play, or dance and sing.

Imani

Kwanzaa is coming to an end. The seventh day is Imani. The principle for this last day means faith. To have faith means to believe in something.

SEVEN CANDLES

On Imani, the family lights all seven candles. Everybody talks about what they believe in, particularly in the wisdom and strength of their parents, teachers, and leaders.

Families exchange Zawadi as part of their Kwanzaa ceremonies. Parents often give their children books of African stories or about African American heroes.

Children are asked to say what faith means to them.

GIVING GIFTS

During Kwanzaa, family members give one another gifts, called Zawadi. The gifts are usually simple and often homemade. Some families give Zawadi every day of Kwanzaa, and others wait until the seventh day to exchange theirs. Children receive gifts to reward them for the promises made during the holiday and for the ones kept from the past year.

THE END OF KWANZAA

The family takes part in the Libation Ceremony. Everybody drinks from the unity cup. Then the candles are put out for the last time. It is the last day of Kwanzaa. Everybody shouts "Harambee! Harambee! Harambee! Harambee! Harambee! Harambee! Harambee!" The new year has begun.

Imani is a good day to go out to public events. Shows, concerts, and fairs for Kwanzaa are held all over the country.

African American Unity Sculpture

27

Let's Celebrate!

Join in the fun! Try making Benne cakes for the Karamu, and your own instrument to play during Kwanzaa.

MAKING BENNE CAKES

ASK AN ADULT TO HELP YOU.
Things you will need:

- greased cookie sheets
- 2 large bowls
- a wooden spoon
- 2 packed cups of brown sugar
- ½ cup softened butter
- 2 eggs, beaten
- 2 cups toasted sesame seeds
- 1 teaspoon vanilla extract
- 2 teaspoons lemon juice
- 1 cup all-purpose flour
- 1 teaspoon baking powder
- ½ teaspoon salt

Directions:

1. Preheat oven to 325 degrees.
2. Beat the sugar and butter together in a large bowl.
3. Stir in the eggs, lemon juice, and vanilla.
4. In another bowl, sift the flour together with baking powder and salt. Stir in the sesame seeds.
5. Gradually add the flour mixture to the other bowl. Stir it in gently.
6. Drop teaspoonfuls of your mixture onto the cookie sheets, 2 inches apart.
7. Bake for 12 to 15 minutes, or until the edges are golden brown.

MAKING A RATTLE DRUM

Materials:

- an empty 11 ½-oz (326-g) coffee can with a plastic lid
- colored paper
- paints or felt-tipped pens
- tape and glue
- dried beans
- a wooden stick or spoon

Directions:

1. Cover the can with a piece of colored paper, and tape or glue it in place.
2. Decorate the can with any patterns or shapes you like. You can stick on pieces of colored paper, or you can use paints and colored pens.
3. Put a few handfuls of dried beans in your decorated can.
4. Replace the lid, and tape it on.
5. Shake your can as a rattle, or use a wooden stick or spoon to beat it like a drum!

Glossary

Ancestors The people in your family who lived before you.

Celebrate To show that a certain day or event is special.

Civil rights The basic freedom that every person should have.

Community A group of people who live and work together.

Custom A way of doing something that follows tradition.

Harvest The time of year when crops are picked and gathered.

Okra A green vegetable often used in soups or stews.

Plantation A large farm where crops are grown and where
      people live and work.

Principle A belief that shows people how to behave.

Symbol Something that stands for an idea.

Tradition A very old way of living that parents teach to their children.

Pronunciation Guide

Habari gani	hah-BAH-ree GAH-nee
Harambee	hah-RAHM-bee
Imani	ee-MAH-nee
Karamu	kah-RAH-moo
Kinara	kee-NAH-rah
Kujichagulia	koo-jee-chah-goo-LEE-ah
Kuumba	koo-OOM-bah
Kwanzaa	KWAN-zah
Nguzo Saba	en-GOO-zoh SAH-bah
Nia	NEE-ah
Ujamaa	oo-jah-MAA
Ujima	oo-JEE-mah
Umoja	oo-MOH-jah
Zawadi	za-WAH-dee

30

Further Reading

Goss, Linda and Clay. *It's Kwanzaa Time!* G. P. Putnam's Sons, 1995.

Johnson, Delores. *The Children's Book of Kwanzaa.* Aladdin, 1997.

Medearis, Angela Shelf. *The Seven Days of Kwanzaa.* Scholastic, 1994.

Pinkney, Andrea Davis. *Seven Candles for Kwanzaa.* Dial, 1993.

Saint James, Synthia. *The Gifts of Kwanzaa.* Albert Whitman & Co., 1994.

Washington, Donna L. *The Story of Kwanzaa.* Harper Collins, 1996.

Index